COOKING THE

THE

MEDITERRANEAN

WAY

Lerner Publications Company
A division of Lerner Publishing Group
241 First Avenue North
Minneapolis, MN 55401 U.S.A.

Website address: www.lernerbooks.com

Library of Congress Cataloging-in-Publication Data

Behnke, Alison.
    Cooking the Mediterranean way / by Alison Behnke, and Anna and Lazaros Christoforides.
        p.   cm. — (Easy menu ethnic cookbooks)
    Includes index.
    ISBN: 0–8225–1237–8 (lib. bdg. : alk. paper)
    1. Cookery, Mediterranean—Juvenile literature. 2. Mediterranean Region—Social life and customs—Juvenile literature. I. Christoforides, Anna. II. Christoforides, Lazaros. III. Title. IV. Series.
TX725.M35B44 2005
641.59'1822—dc22   2004011054

Manufactured in the United States of America
1 2 3 4 5 6 – JR – 10 09 08 07 06 05

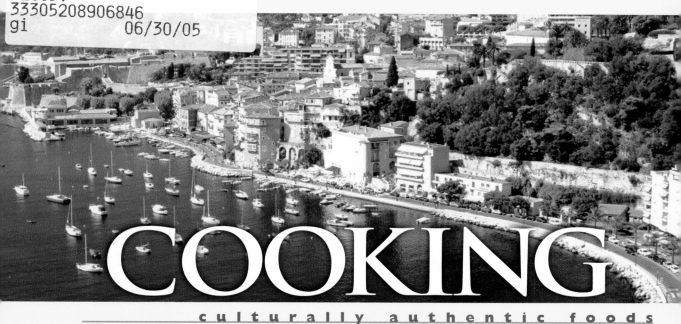

...u ethnic cookbooks

COOKING

culturally authentic foods

THE

including low-fat and

MEDITERRANEAN

vegetarian recipes

WAY

Alison Behnke in consultation with Anna and Lazaros Christoforides

...ons Company • Minneapolis

Contents

Introduction

The word *Mediterranean* evokes images of blue skies, warm sun and, above all, the sparkling waves of the Mediterranean Sea. The region is rich with natural beauty, along with a fascinating history and culture.

For travelers and readers with an appetite, the Mediterranean also summons thoughts of wonderful food. Blessed with a mild climate and fertile soil, the farms and orchards of the region produce a wealth of fresh, delicious grains, vegetables, and fruits, while miles of coastline provide fishing crews with generous catches of fresh seafood. From delectable Lebanese meze (appetizers), flavored with garlic, lemon, and mint, to Italy's pastas and pizzas, to the rich lamb dishes of Morocco, the Mediterranean is truly a diner's delight.

Fresh produce and vivid colors are common in Mediterranean cooking. This French recipe for stuffed tomatoes features fresh tomatoes and herbs. (Recipe on page 38.)

The History and Land

The Mediterranean is a unique and fascinating geographical region, with more than a dozen countries in Europe, Africa, and Asia. Connected by the common body of water, the Mediterranean Sea, the nations that lie along the shores of the Mediterranean are Spain, France, Italy, Albania, Greece, Turkey, Syria, Lebanon, Israel, Egypt, Libya, Tunisia, Algeria, and Morocco. Major islands such as Corsica, Crete, Cyprus, Malta, and Sicily dot the sea. These lands also comprise a rich historical region, tied together by intertwining threads of exploration, invasion, and trade. Parts of the region were settled more than ten thousand years ago, when early hunting, fishing, and gathering cultures sprang up near the water's edge. More advanced civilizations gradually grew out of these first societies. The Greeks controlled vast holdings along all the coasts of the Mediterranean more than two thousand years ago, followed by the Romans. Other major powers in various parts of the region have included the empires of the Spanish, French, Turks, and British. Just as each of these groups left its mark on the area's architecture, language, and culture, each also made contributions to the Mediterranean's varied and delicious cuisine.

The Mediterranean region's topography is also an important part of its identity. Most of the nations that lie on the sea's northern and eastern shores have dramatic landscapes, with interior mountains or hills that slope down to coastal plains. To the south, western North Africa shares this topography, while countries lying farther east, such as Algeria, Libya, and Egypt, are somewhat flatter and dominated by expanses of desert. And with sunny, dry summers and cooler, rainier winters, the Mediterranean is renowned for its pleasant, mild climate.

The warm climate and agricultural bounty help define the typical local foods of each nation along the sea's shores. In Spain's southern and eastern regions, for example, local markets are filled with olives, citrus fruits, rice, onions, and potatoes. The farmers of France's coastal southern regions of Provence and the Côte d'Azur raise vegetable crops such as bright purple eggplants and red, yellow, orange, and green bell peppers. Members of the squash family, such as *courgettes* (zucchini) and pumpkins, are also part of local harvests. Farther east, Italy—a peninsula jutting into the waters of the Mediterranean— produces delectable crops of fruits such as grapes, oranges, and lemons, along with fresh herbs including basil, Italian parsley, and rosemary. Sicily, a large island at Italy's southern tip, boasts fresh, flavorful foods, such as artichokes, juicy tomatoes, radishes, fennel,

A worker uses a tarp to gather harvested olives in Tuscany, a region in west-central Italy.

and eggplant. In the northeastern Mediterranean lie Greece and Turkey, where olives are the most important crop. Squid and octopus are popular choices for seafood on most of the Greek islands, while many Turkish diners prefer sea bass, mackerel, and other types of fish.

Along the Mediterranean's eastern edge, somewhat drier, warmer weather favors crops such as olives and barley. Lebanon is known for its juicy lemons, while Syrian harvests include staples such as lentils and chickpeas. Here and to the north in Greece and Turkey, honey and locally raised nuts flavor rich desserts.

The southern waters that lap the shores of North Africa find a hotter climate but still enough rainfall to grow a number of important foods. Egypt produces rice, corn, and beans, while Moroccan and

Libyan farms raise wheat and barley. Tomatoes and almonds are part of Tunisian harvests, and olives and dates are grown throughout the area. In addition, nomadic herders drive goats and sheep across the land, and meat from these animals figures prominently in the regional diet.

The Food

Although eating habits vary from country to country, Mediterranean diners generally eat light breakfasts. In Greece, for example, the morning meal often consists of thick, strong coffee—which some people like very sweet—and a piece of bread with olive oil, butter, cheese, jam, or honey. Similar breakfasts start the day for many people in Italy, Spain, and France, while in the eastern Mediterranean, typical breakfasts consist of sweet coffee, pita bread, yogurt, and fruit. People in North Africa also commonly have flat bread, often accompanied by cheese, yogurt, beans, or porridge and dates or other fruit.

Traditionally, many diners on all sides of the Mediterranean enjoyed a large midday meal, often followed by an afternoon rest—called a siesta in Italy and Spain—to escape the day's harshest heat. Although some families still gather for large, leisurely lunches, modern work schedules and school days have led many people to save the day's main meal for the evening.

Most people in the northern Mediterranean eat supper late, often sitting down to the meal at 9:00 P.M. or even later. These meals may have many courses, and children sometimes head off to bed while the adults are still around the table, chatting and enjoying tea or coffee.

As diverse as the countries surrounding the Mediterranean are, their similar climate and common history have led to noticeable similarities among their cuisines. Garlic, tomatoes, almonds, and rice are a few of the ingredients that show up over and over again in regional recipes. Many dishes are eaten in a wide range of nations, although local cooks usually add their own twist to the preparation, and each nation's influence is evident through its cooking.

For example, an Arab influence in Sicily has produced local specialties such as *fagioli alla menta*, a hearty dish of white beans, celery, garlic, and mint. Sicily's southern locale has also given diners there the spiciest palates in Italy, and simple pasta dishes dressed with fiery tomato and hot pepper sauces—often flavored with anchovy paste—are island standards. More typically, Italian dishes include lasagna, *pasta alla Norma* (pasta with tomatoes, eggplant, and ricotta cheese), polenta (cornmeal porridge) and calamari, fresh squid served sautéed or deep-fried.

Corsica, another island off Italy's coast, is actually part of France's territory, and its specialties reflect both French and Italian tastes. A popular bean and vegetable soup is very similar to the Italian minestrone, while a wide variety of pâtés (meat spreads) are typically French. Various pork sausages and goat's or ewe's milk cheese are the pride of Corsican groceries. Chestnuts are also an abundant local crop. A chestnut soup made with goat's milk and a version of polenta made with chestnut flour instead of cornmeal are frequently found on island tables.

The island of Cyprus, lying in the far eastern Mediterranean, is one of the most dramatic examples of cultural blending in the region. The northern portion of the island, claimed by Turkey, show-cases Turkish favorites such as *bulgur pilav*, a dish of seasoned cracked wheat often served with yogurt. The cooks of southern Cyprus, which is occupied primarily by Greeks, offer Greek dishes, such as moussaka (layered eggplant and beef or lamb baked in a rich sauce). A more unique Cypriot specialty is *halloumi*, a soft cheese made from goat's and sheep's milk that is often eaten fried or grilled and served with the Mediterranean flat bread called pita.

Fish and seafood, of course, are common ingredients in nearly all the region's cuisines. They appear in dishes from Spanish paella—tomato-and-saffron-flavored rice with clams, shrimp, and often meat—to *aljotta*, the classic fish soup of Malta. Sicilian seafood favorites include *tonno 'nfurnatu* (baked tuna with olives, tomatoes, and capers) and *agghiotta di pesce spada* (swordfish with pine nuts, golden raisins, basil, and tomatoes).

In North Africa, red meat and chicken feature more prominently in favorite dishes, such as *kefta* (grilled lamb or beef meatballs) and tagines (stews). Couscous—small, pastalike pellets made from a grain in the wheat family—is the most common accompaniment to North African entrées. Glasses of hot, sweet mint tea often follow a meal in North Africa. Other typical beverages around the Mediterranean include sweet Lebanese lemonade made from local fruit; almond milk in Spain, Italy, and the Middle East; and *ayran*, a refreshing yogurt drink popular in Turkey.

Mediterranean diners also have a sweet tooth. In Greece, Turkey, and the Middle East, a typical dessert is the rich, sweet baklava, made with thin phyllo dough, butter, honey, and chopped walnuts, pistachios, or other nuts. Halvah, made from honey and ground

A Moroccan man serves mint tea, a popular North African beverage.

13

sesame seeds, is another favorite sweet in the eastern Mediterranean. In North Africa, dates are a major part of desserts including *makroudh*, filled cookies drenched in a sugary syrup.

Across the Strait of Gibraltar from Morocco, Spanish diners enjoy rich desserts such as rice pudding and *crema catalan*, a cold custard with a crisp, sugary surface. French cooks prepare delicate sweet pancakes called crêpes, with fillings such as fruit, chestnut paste, or chocolate. And throughout the region, fresh fruit is a perfect finish to any meal.

Holidays and Festivals

The many cultures of the Mediterranean celebrate a wide variety of holidays and festivals. Many of these special events are religious in nature, and they reflect the region's long history and great diversity. Most also have special foods associated with them.

For Christians, who live primarily in the northern Mediterranean and parts of the Middle East, Easter and Christmas are the year's biggest holidays. Lebanese Christians begin their celebration of Easter on Palm Sunday (the Sunday before Easter), when families carry palm leaves and flowers through the streets to commemorate Jesus' procession through Jerusalem several days before his crucifixion. Easter celebrates Jesus' rise from the dead following his crucifixion, and the day is marked with great feasts that always include *maamoul*, a sweet pastry stuffed with dates or nuts. In Malta the traditional Easter sweets are *figolli*, cookielike confections filled with almond paste. On the Greek island of Crete, where many residents follow the Greek Orthodox branch of Christianity, worshippers attend a midnight service the night before Easter. Afterward, members of the congregation use candles to light the streets on their way home, while fireworks light the sky overhead. The next day, many Greeks enjoy buttery, crescent-shaped cookies called *kourabiéthes*.

Christmas festivities are also held throughout the region. French families attend midnight church services on Christmas Eve and return home to *le réveillon*, a late meal of many courses. The feast may include roast goose or turkey, oysters, salads, and fruit. Dessert is often the traditional *bûche de Noël*, a rich log-shaped cake filled with chocolate or chestnut-flavored cream. Before bed, children in southern France leave their shoes out, hoping they will be filled with candy, nuts, and other gifts from Père Noël (Father Christmas). In Syria the nation's small Christian population has its own holiday traditions. Christmas Eve bonfires are a favorite custom. After church on Christmas morning, families share meals that may include turkey, roast duck, and rich sweets. At Epiphany, which falls a few days after Christmas and celebrates a visit to baby Jesus by three kings bearing gifts, the Christmas camel brings gifts to good children.

Jewish populations in Israel and throughout the region observe a variety of important religious holidays, and each is associated with special foods. At Rosh Hashanah, the Jewish New Year, diners enjoy a traditional bread called challah. Although challah is usually braided, it is made in round loaves for Rosh Hashanah to represent the year's cycle. Passover, marking the end of the Hebrews' slavery in Egypt, is celebrated with a great feast that includes specific ceremonial foods, such as bitter herbs, roasted eggs, and matzo (flat, unleavened bread). The dessert at this meal is a cake made of matzo. The matzo symbolizes the haste of the Hebrew families as they fled their enslavement in ancient Egypt.

Shavuot is observed in honor of the biblical figure Moses receiving the Ten Commandments from God. This holiday is celebrated with a variety of dairy foods such as milk and different cheeses, while meat and fish are avoided. Popular Shavuot dishes include blintzes—thin pancakes filled with sweetened cottage cheese or farmers' cheese.

For other special occasions, Jewish communities in Algeria, Morocco, and other parts of French-speaking North Africa adapt local

During Ramadan, strings of lights decorate the gate to the Muslim Quarter of Jerusalem.

foods to festival traditions. Many cooks in these countries serve a sweet, buttery version of couscous called *couscous au beurre* for holidays.

Most residents of North Africa and much of the Middle East are Muslims (followers of Islam). The holy month of Ramadan is one of the most sacred times of the year for Muslims, who observe it by fasting. While fasting, they eat nothing between sunrise and sunset. The month is a time for prayer, services at mosques (Islamic places of worship), and quiet contemplation. However, it is also a festive time. After dark, a meal called the *iftar* breaks each day's fast, and friends and families often meet to share this evening meal. Egyptians listen to storytellers and musicians in public squares as the sun sets. In some countries, the streets are strung with colored lights and tents are set up where people gather to dine and celebrate. Many people end the day's fast by eating dates. It is believed that Muhammad, Islam's founding prophet, always broke his fast with dates. In Morocco and other parts of North Africa, Muslims commonly eat *harira*, a nutritious soup of meat, lentils, and chickpeas, for the iftar. The end of Ramadan is celebrated with a magnificent three-day feast and festival called Eid al-Fitr.

Eid al-Adha is another important Islamic holiday. The festival commemorates a story in the Quran (Islam's holy book). In the story, God asks Abraham, one of his followers, to prove his devotion to God by sacrificing his son. As Abraham is about to obey, God rewards him for his faith by telling him to release his son and sacrifice a sheep instead. Eid al-Adha takes place at the time of the annual hajj, a pilgrimage to the Islamic holy city of Mecca, Saudi Arabia. Muslims traditionally roast a sheep and share the meat with friends and neighbors. In Turkey, where the holiday is called Kurban Bayrami, families usually sacrifice a sheep in the morning, giving some of the meat to charity and preparing the rest for a large meal later in the day.

Festivals giving thanks for bountiful harvests are also a centuries-old tradition throughout the Mediterranean, and festivalgoers typically enjoy many dishes featuring the celebrated food. In Israel the festival of Sukkot was originally in honor of the grape and other fruit harvests. Similar events in Algeria and Morocco star local produce such as dates, tomatoes, and cherries, and the island of Cyprus hosts watermelon and orange festivals. Assi Gonia, Greece, holds a springtime festival, when dozens of local shepherds drive their flocks to the central square to be sheared. Afterward, many people enjoy dishes made with fresh sheep's milk. In Malta a summer harvest-end tradition is the *fenekata*, a day of singing, dancing, and feasting on rabbit dishes.

Before You Begin

Mediterranean cooking uses some ingredients that you may not know. Sometimes special cookware is used too, although the recipes in this book can easily be prepared with ordinary utensils and pans.

The most important thing you need to know before you start is how to be a careful cook. On the following page, you'll find a few rules that will make your cooking experience safe, fun, and easy. Next, take a look at the "dictionary" of utensils, terms, and special ingredients. You may also want to read the list of tips on preparing healthy, low-fat meals.

When you've picked out a recipe to try, read through it from beginning to end. Then you are ready to shop for ingredients and to organize the cookware you will need. Once you have assembled everything, you're ready to begin cooking.

This hearty North African stew of chicken and apricots can be served with rice or couscous. (Recipe on page 48.)

The Careful Cook

Whenever you cook, there are certain safety rules you must always keep in mind. Even experienced cooks follow these rules when they are in the kitchen.

- Always wash your hands before handling food. Thoroughly wash all raw vegetables and fruits to remove dirt, chemicals, and insecticides.
- Wash uncooked poultry, fish, and meat under cold water.
- Use a cutting board when cutting up vegetables and fruits. Don't cut them up in your hand! And be sure to cut in a direction *away* from you and your fingers.
- Long hair or loose clothing can easily catch fire if brought near the burners of a stove. If you have long hair, tie it back before you start cooking.
- Turn all pot handles toward the back of the stove so that you will not catch your sleeves or jewelry on them. This is especially important when younger brothers and sisters are around. They could easily knock off a pot and get burned.
- Always use a pot holder to steady hot pots or to take pans out of the oven. Don't use a wet cloth on a hot pan because the steam it produces could burn you.
- Lift the lid of a steaming pot with the opening away from you so you will not get burned.
- If you get burned, hold the burn under cold running water. Do not put grease or butter on it. Cold water helps to take the heat out, but grease or butter will only keep it in.
- If grease or cooking oil catches fire, throw baking soda or salt at the bottom of the flame to put it out. (Water will *not* put out a grease fire.) Call for help, and try to turn all the stove burners to "off."

Cooking Utensils

colander—A bowl-shaped dish with holes in it that is used for washing or draining food

mortar—A strong bowl used, with a pestle, to grind, crush, or mash spices and other foods

pastry bag—A cone-shaped bag made of cloth, nylon, or plastic. A filling or frosting is inserted through the wide end of the bag, and it is squeezed through the narrow tip.

pestle—A club-shaped utensil used with a mortar to grind, crush, or mash spices or other foods

skewer—A thin wooden or metal rod used to hold small pieces of food for broiling or grilling

stockpot—a large, heavy pot, often used for cooking soups

Cooking Terms

broil—To cook food directly under a heat source so that the side facing the heat cooks rapidly

brown—To cook food quickly over high heat so that the surface turns an even brown

cream—To stir or beat one or several ingredients to a smooth consistency

grate—To cut food into tiny pieces by rubbing it against a grater

knead—To work dough or other thick mixture by pressing it with the palms, pushing it outward and then pressing it over on itself

pinch—A very small amount, usually what you can pick up between your thumb and first finger

preheat—To allow an oven to warm up to a certain temperature before putting food in it

pulse—To chop, mix, or blend by turning a food processor on and off in rapid succession

sauté—To fry quickly over high heat in oil or butter, stirring or turning the food to prevent burning

seed—To remove seeds from a food

shred—To tear into small pieces, either by hand or with a grater

sift—To mix several dry ingredients together or to remove lumps in dry ingredients by putting them through a sieve or sifter

simmer—To cook over low heat in liquid kept just below its boiling point. Bubbles may occasionally rise to the surface.

Special Ingredients

basil—A fragrant herb whose fresh or dried leaves are used in cooking

bouillon cubes—Flavored cubes that can be used to make beef, chicken, fish, or vegetable stock

candied orange peel—Sugared strips of orange peel. Candied orange peel is available in supermarkets and Italian specialty stores.

cayenne pepper— Dried red chilies (hot peppers) ground to a fine powder. Cayenne adds a very spicy flavor to foods.

chickpeas—A type of legume with a nutlike flavor. Chickpeas are also called garbanzo beans and are available dried or canned.

coriander—An herb used ground as a flavoring or fresh as a garnish. Fresh coriander is also known as cilantro.

couscous—Semolina wheat, traditionally rolled by hand into small grains or pellets

cumin—The ground seeds of an herb in the parsley family, used in cooking to give food a slightly hot flavor

dates—Small brown fruits of a tropical palm tree that have very sweet, tender flesh. They are often dried and used for eating and cooking.

dill—An herb whose seeds and leaves are both used in cooking. Dried dill is also called dill weed.

feta cheese—A crumbly white cheese made from goat's or sheep's milk

grape leaves—Leaves from grapevine plants, usually found packed in jars with brine (salt water) and used throughout the Mediterranean to make rolls filled with meat or rice

great northern beans—Large white beans that can be bought dried or canned

halloumi cheese—A soft white cheese made from sheep's or goat's milk and flavored with mint and salt water. Halloumi is originally from Cyprus.

marjoram—An herb related to mint that is used in cooking. It is known for its sweet aroma and flavor.

oregano—A pungent herb in the mint family, used fresh or dried—and either whole or ground—as a seasoning

paprika—Dried ground sweet red peppers. Paprika is used for both its flavor and its red color.

pine nut—The edible seed of certain pine trees

pita bread—Flat, round pieces of bread. When baked, a pocket of air forms in the center of the bread.

ricotta cheese—A white cheese, made with whole or skim milk, that resembles cottage cheese

ricotta salata—Dried, salted ricotta cheese

rosemary—An herb in the mint family that has needlelike leaves and a sharp flavor

saffron—A spice, made from part of a crocus flower, that adds flavor and a yellow color to foods. It is available in threads or in a powdered form. If saffron is too expensive, Mediterranean cooks often use turmeric instead.

scallions—A variety of green onion

semolina flour—Coarse flour made from the gritty, grainlike portions of hard wheat

thyme—A fragrant herb used fresh or dry to season foods

turmeric—An aromatic spice that gives a bright yellow color to foods

Healthy and Low-Fat Cooking Tips

Many modern cooks are concerned about preparing healthy, low-fat meals. The Mediterranean region is widely considered to be the home of one of the world's healthiest cuisines, but you can still use a few simple methods to reduce the fat content of most dishes. Here are a few general tips for adapting the recipes in this book. Throughout the book, you'll also find specific suggestions for individual recipes—and don't worry, they'll still taste delicious!

Olive oil is a staple of Mediterranean cooking. It is more heart-healthy than butter, margarine, or many other cooking oils. However, it is high in fat. It is often a good idea to prepare the recipe as written the first time, but once you are familiar with the original, you may want to experiment with reducing the amount of oil that you use. In some recipes, where oil is used to coat cookware, you can substitute a low-fat or nonfat cooking spray.

Meat can be another source of unwanted fat, although many Mediterranean recipes are meatless. Buying extra-lean meats and trimming as much fat as possible is also an easy way to reduce fat. You may choose to omit meat altogether from some recipes. Replacing meat with hearty vegetables, such as potatoes or eggplant, or with meat substitutes, such as tofu or tempeh (soybean products), can keep your dishes filling and satisfying.

There are also many ways to reduce fat added by cheese and other dairy products. Local cheeses are featured in a wide variety of Mediterranean dishes, but by simply using less than called for, you can quickly lower a meal's fat content. Use low-fat or nonfat milk, buttermilk, and yogurt to cut fat grams even further.

There are many ways to prepare meals that are good for you and still taste great. As you become a more experienced cook, you will find the methods that work best for you.

METRIC CONVERSIONS

Cooks in the United States measure both liquid and solid ingredients using standard containers based on the 8-ounce cup and the tablespoon. These measurements are based on volume, while the metric system of measurement is based on both weight (for solids) and volume (for liquids). To convert from U.S. fluid tablespoons, ounces, quarts, and so forth to metric liters is a straightforward conversion, using the chart below. However, since solids have different weights—one cup of rice does not weigh the same as one cup of grated cheese, for example—many cooks who use the metric system have kitchen scales to weigh different ingredients. The chart below will give you a good starting point for basic conversions to the metric system.

MASS (weight)

1 ounce (oz.)	=	28.0 grams (g)
8 ounces	=	227.0 grams
1 pound (lb.) or 16 ounces	=	0.45 kilograms (kg)
2.2 pounds	=	1.0 kilogram

LIQUID VOLUME

1 teaspoon (tsp.)	=	5.0 milliliters (ml)
1 tablespoon (tbsp.)	=	15.0 milliliters
1 fluid ounce (oz.)	=	30.0 milliliters
1 cup (c.)	=	240 milliliters
1 pint (pt.)	=	480 milliliters
1 quart (qt.)	=	0.95 liters (l)
1 gallon (gal.)	=	3.80 liters

LENGTH

¼ inch (in.)	=	0.6 centimeters (cm)
½ inch	=	1.25 centimeters
1 inch	=	2.5 centimeters

TEMPERATURE

212°F	=	100°C (boiling point of water)
225°F	=	110°C
250°F	=	120°C
275°F	=	135°C
300°F	=	150°C
325°F	=	160°C
350°F	=	180°C
375°F	=	190°C
400°F	=	200°C

(To convert temperature in Fahrenheit to Celsius, subtract 32 and multiply by .56)

PAN SIZES

8-inch cake pan	=	20 x 4-centimeter cake pan
9-inch cake pan	=	23 x 3.5-centimeter cake pan
11 x 7-inch baking pan	=	28 x 18-centimeter baking pan
13 x 9-inch baking pan	=	32.5 x 23-centimeter baking pan
9 x 5-inch loaf pan	=	23 x 13-centimeter loaf pan
2-quart casserole	=	2-liter casserole

A Mediterranean Table

In as vast and varied a region as the Mediterranean, it's no surprise that there is an equally varied range of mealtime customs. From traditional Moroccan meals—at which diners sit on large pillows and eat at low tables covered with bright, richly decorated cloths—to formal French dinners—with white tablecloths, candles, and folded cloth napkins—there are as many ways to enjoy a Mediterranean meal as there are Mediterranean countries.

However, the common theme that ties all Mediterranean tables together is a focus on fresh, seasonal ingredients. Every Mediterranean cook knows the best time to buy his or her favorite produce and grains at local markets. The creative, skillful, and healthy preparation of these fresh goods is an integral part of all Mediterranean cooking.

Guests at a Kurdish wedding in Turkey enjoy a traditional wedding feast. Kurds are an ethnic group whose historic homeland stretches across parts of Turkey, Syria, Iran, and Iraq.

A Mediterranean Menu

Below are suggested menus for two typical Mediterranean meals, drawing upon the region's many diverse specialties. Also included are shopping lists of the ingredients you'll need to prepare these meals. These are just a few possible combinations of dishes and flavors. As you gain more experience with Mediterranean cooking, you may enjoy planning your own menus.

LUNCH

Baked rice

Mediterranean fruit salad

Yogurt drink

SHOPPING LIST:

Produce

2 medium potatoes
1 head garlic
2 medium tomatoes
1 melon
2 pears
2 apples
2 oranges
½ lb. strawberries
1 medium bunch grapes

Dairy/Egg/Meat

2 links Spanish chorizo or a milder pork sausage
32 oz. plain yogurt

Canned/Bottled/Boxed

12 oz. canned chickpeas
32 oz. canned chicken or beef broth, or 4 bouillon cubes
olive oil

Miscellaneous

short-grain rice, such as Arborio
paprika
saffron
salt

SUPPER

Stuffed tomatoes

Chicken and apricot
stew

Date-filled pastries

Mint tea

SHOPPING LIST:

Produce

2 small yellow onions
4 cloves garlic
4 medium tomatoes
1 orange
3 to 4 c. fresh parsley or
    basil
1 bunch fresh mint leaves

Dairy/Egg/Meat

2 lb. skinless, boneless
    chicken breasts and thighs
2 sticks unsalted butter

Canned/Bottled/Boxed

vegetable oil
olive oil
honey

Miscellaneous

couscous or rice
3 c. semolina flour
2 c. pitted dates
1 c. dried apricots
baking soda
cinnamon
turmeric
saffron
salt
pepper
sugar cubes or white sugar
loose-leaf green tea

Starters, Salads, and Sides

Appetizers and side dishes are one of the best ways to sample a wide variety of Mediterranean cuisine—without filling up too fast. In many of the region's nations, a lavish spread of appetizers is a tasty beginning to lunch or dinner. And from fresh-tasting, garlicky Greek spreads to heavily spiced Moroccan meatballs fresh from the grill, these dishes offer flavors to tempt every diner.

Hearty salads from the region, such as the Spanish *empedrat* made with beans and tuna fish, make perfect complements to many Mediterranean entrées. These dishes can also be served with a slice of crusty bread or warm pita to make a satisfying light lunch. In addition, vegetable side dishes nicely round out any meal, whether the main course is meat or vegetarian.

Skewers of spicy grilled meatballs make a tasty Moroccan appetizer. (Recipe on page 32.)

Grilled Meatballs/Kefta (Morocco)

These spicy meatballs are usually grilled in Morocco,* but they can also be broiled in the oven or fried in a pan with a small amount of vegetable or olive oil. If you choose to grill your kefta, make sure that you have an adult to help you.

1 lb. ground lamb or beef

1 small onion, chopped finely

1½ tbsp. fresh parsley, chopped

¾ tsp. salt

¾ tsp. cumin

½ tsp. pepper

½ tsp. coriander

½ tsp. dried mint

¼ tsp. cayenne

¼ tsp. marjoram

¼ tsp. paprika

*Kefta is also a popular dish in Greece and Turkey. For meatballs with the flavor of the eastern Mediterranean, omit the cumin, coriander, cayenne, marjoram, and paprika and replace them with 1 tsp. oregano, 2 cloves minced garlic, and ½ c. bread crumbs.

1. Place 10 to 15 flat bamboo skewers in a wide pan or baking dish full of water to soak. Or if you have metal skewers, skip this step.

2. Combine all ingredients in a large bowl. Mix well. Cover and refrigerate for at least 1 hour.

3. Have an experienced cook start a charcoal or gas grill, if using.

4. Remove skewers from water. Wet your hands with a little bit of water. Form meat mixture into 2-inch-long oval-shaped patties and carefully thread 2 to 3 patties onto each skewer. Flatten patties slightly so they will not roll.

5. Set the oven, if using, to broil.

6. Grill or broil the skewers for 6 to 10 minutes total, turning once, until meat is cooked through.

7. Remove skewers to a serving platter and serve hot.

Preparation time: 20 to 25 minutes
(plus 1 hour chilling time)
Cooking time: 6 to 10 minutes
Serves 6 to 8

Cucumber and Yogurt Dip / Tzatziki (Greece)

1 large cucumber, peeled, seeded, and grated*

2 tsp. salt

2 c. plain low-fat or nonfat yogurt, drained**

4 cloves garlic, minced

3 tbsp. olive oil

1 tsp. lemon juice

1 tsp. pepper

1. Sprinkle grated cucumber with salt and leave in a colander to drain for 30 minutes. Meanwhile, combine yogurt, garlic, olive oil, lemon juice, and pepper in a large bowl. Cover and refrigerate while cucumber drains.

2. Use your hands to squeeze cucumber dry and stir gently into yogurt mixture.

Preparation time: 40 minutes
(plus overnight draining time)
Serves 6

*To seed a cucumber, slice the cucumber in half lengthwise. Hold the cucumber, cut side up, with one hand while using a small spoon to scrape out seeds.

**To drain yogurt, place it in a strainer lined with a coffee filter or cheesecloth and placed over a bowl. Put the bowl in the refrigerator overnight. In the morning, remove the yogurt from the strainer and discard the liquid in the bowl below.

Spicy Cheese Spread / Tirokafteri (Greece)

2 c. crumbled feta cheese

6 to 8 tbsp. olive oil

2 hot peppers, seeded and chopped***

1. Combine all ingredients in a food processor or blender. Process until smooth (add more or less olive oil depending on the consistency you prefer).

Preparation time: 10 minutes
Serves 6

***Depending on how spicy you'd like your tirokafteri, you may use a relatively mild hot pepper such as pepperoncini or a hotter variety such as jalapeño. You'll also want to be careful when working with hot peppers. Wear rubber gloves while cutting the pepper and be sure to remove all the seeds. Wash your hands well when you are done.

White Bean and Tuna Salad/Empedrat (Spain)

This traditional dish from Spain's northeastern province of Catalonia brings together some of Spanish cooking's classic ingredients: beans, olives, and fish.

1 15½-oz. can great northern beans, drained

1 6-oz. can tuna fish in water, drained

1 medium white onion, chopped

2 tomatoes, chopped

½ c. sliced black olives

2 hard-cooked eggs, chopped (optional)*

4 tbsp. olive oil

1 tbsp. white vinegar

¾ tsp. salt

¼ tsp. pepper

1. In a large bowl, combine beans, tuna, onion, tomatoes, olives, and eggs (if using).

2. In a smaller bowl, combine olive oil, vinegar, salt, and pepper. Stir well to blend.

3. Pour olive oil mixture over salad and mix carefully. Refrigerate 1 hour before serving.

Preparation time: 25 minutes
(plus 1 hour chilling time)
Serves 4

*To hard-cook eggs, place them in a saucepan and cover with cold water. Place over medium heat until boiling, reduce heat, and simmer for 15 minutes. Drain water from saucepan and run cold water over eggs until they are cool. Peel and chop eggs.

Bulgur Salad / Tabbouleh
(Lebanon, Syria, Israel, Turkey)

Bulgur is one of the most popular grains in the eastern Mediterranean. This refreshing, flavorful salad is typically associated with Lebanese cooking, but it is also popular in Turkey, Syria, and Israel.

2 c. bulgur*

1 onion, peeled and finely chopped

4 large tomatoes, chopped

2 bunches scallions, finely chopped
(about 1 c.)

2 small cucumbers, peeled and
chopped

½ c. olive oil

juice of 2 lemons (about 6 tbsp.)

1 tsp. salt

¼ tsp. pepper

6 tbsp. chopped fresh parsley

3 tbsp. chopped fresh mint, or
1 tbsp. dried mint

1. In a medium saucepan, bring 2 c. water to a boil. Remove from heat, add bulgur, and cover for 20 minutes.

2. In a large mixing bowl, combine bulgur with all remaining ingredients.

3. Place mixture in a large serving bowl. Chill several hours before serving.

Preparation time: 25 minutes (plus several hours chilling time)
Serves 4 to 6

*Look for bulgur in the bulk food section of your supermarket or grocery store. If the store doesn't carry it, check at health food stores or try specialty Middle Eastern markets. You may also substitute cracked wheat for bulgur.

Stuffed Tomatoes/ *Tomates Farcies (France)*

Fresh tomatoes are often prepared simply to bring out their natural flavor. To make this attractive salad or side dish, use the reddest, juiciest tomatoes you can find.

4 medium tomatoes

3 cloves garlic

4 tbsp. olive oil

¾ tsp. salt

¼ tsp. pepper

3 to 4 cups fresh parsley or basil, shredded

1. Cut the tops off tomatoes and use a spoon to scoop out the seeds and pulp inside. Be careful not to break through the tomato skins.

2. Using a large mortar and pestle, or a medium bowl and the back of a spoon, mash the garlic, olive oil, salt, and pepper together. Add parsley or basil and mash to combine well.

3. Fill tomatoes with garlic and herb mixture. Refrigerate for 2 to 3 hours and serve cold.

Preparation time: 10 to 15 minutes
(plus 2 to 3 hours chilling time)
Serves 4

Roasted Potatoes/ *Patate al Forno* (Italy)

Potatoes, oven-roasted with herbs, are a favorite side dish in many Mediterranean countries. This version, with rosemary, is typically Italian. However, you can easily adjust the dish's seasonings to reflect the flavors of other regional cuisines.*

4 to 6 large baking potatoes**

1 tsp. salt

¼ tsp. pepper

4 to 6 tbsp. olive oil

3 to 4 tbsp. chopped fresh rosemary, or 2 tbsp. dried rosemary

1. Preheat oven to 350°F.

2. Cut potatoes into 1-inch chunks. Sprinkle with salt and pepper and toss with olive oil. Place in a glass baking dish or roasting pan, spreading potatoes evenly to form one or two layers.

3. Place in oven and roast for 45 minutes, or until golden brown. Remove from oven, add rosemary, and toss carefully. Return dish to oven and roast five minutes more. Serve hot.

Preparation time: 20 minutes
Cooking time: 50 minutes
Serves 4 to 6

*For a Greek flavor, replace the rosemary with oregano and a sprinkling of 1 or 2 tsp. fresh lemon juice in Step 3. And for a French taste, replace the rosemary with thyme. To prepare roasted potatoes Maltese-style, slice the potatoes rather than chunking, and layer them with thin slices of onion before baking.

**You may peel the potatoes if you prefer, but it isn't necessary.

Main Dishes

Not surprisingly, fish and seafood are among the most common ingredients in Mediterranean entrées, especially in the northern and eastern parts of the region. Seafood dishes are often paired with rice. Rice is featured in many other dishes, as well, and pasta is an important ingredient in Italy.

Couscous is more common than rice in the southern Mediterranean, where dishes often feature lamb or chicken. Soups and stews, such as the rich chicken and apricot stew served in North Africa, are popular main dishes throughout the region and can make a good lunch or dinner.

Yet another Mediterranean specialty is the famous Israeli blintz, which can be easily adapted to any meal or any course. Blintzes are commonly filled with sweetened cheese but may also be stuffed with savory fillings, such as potatoes, or dessert ingredients, such as fruit.

Stuffed grape leaves are a favorite across much of the Mediterranean region. (Recipe on page 50.)

Fish Soup/Aljotta (Malta)

Maltese fishing crews bring in daily catches that include swordfish, sea bass, mullet, white bream, and a local fish called lampuki. When making this traditional garlicky soup, you can use any firm white fish that you like, such as snapper, cod, sole, haddock, or flounder.

2 tbsp. olive oil

2 medium onions, chopped

8 cloves garlic, minced

4 medium tomatoes, peeled and chopped*

2 to 4 sprigs fresh mint, chopped, or 1 tsp. dried mint

2 to 4 sprigs fresh marjoram, chopped, or 1 tsp. dried marjoram

1 tsp. salt

¼ tsp. pepper

10 c. water or fish stock made from bouillon

1 lb. fish fillets

1. Heat oil over medium heat in a large stockpot. Add onion and garlic and sauté 5 to 10 minutes, or until soft but not brown.

2. Add tomatoes, mint, marjoram, salt, pepper, and water or fish stock to pot. Mix well and bring to a boil. Add fish. Reduce heat to medium and simmer 15 minutes, or until fish is cooked all the way through. If desired, remove fillets, cut into bite-sized pieces, and return to soup before serving hot.

Preparation time: 25 minutes
Cooking time: 25 minutes
Serves 4

*To peel a tomato, carefully cut X-shaped slits on the top and bottom of the tomato. Using a slotted spoon, lower the tomato into boiling water and allow to sit for up to 30 seconds. Remove. When the tomato is cool enough to handle, peel off the skin with your fingers.

Baked Rice / Arroz al Horno (Spain)

Rice is a staple ingredient in southeastern Spain, and local cooks prepare a variety of dishes with the versatile grain. Arroz al horno makes a perfect entrée on a chilly night.

1 tbsp. olive oil

2 links Spanish chorizo or a milder pork sausage, cut into quarters*

2 medium potatoes, peeled and thickly sliced

1 whole head garlic, with outermost skin removed

2 medium tomatoes, cut into wedges

2 c. short-grain rice, such as Arborio

1½ c. canned chickpeas, drained

4 c. chicken or beef broth*

1 tsp. paprika

pinch saffron (optional)

½ tsp. salt

*For a vegetarian entrée, simply omit the chorizo and replace the chicken or beef broth with water or vegetable stock.

1. Preheat oven to 400°F.

2. In a deep, wide skillet, heat oil over medium heat. Add sausage and potatoes and sauté 5 minutes, or until lightly browned.

3. Add whole head garlic to pan and sauté 2 to 3 minutes. Add tomato wedges to pan and sauté another 2 to 3 minutes. Remove from heat and set aside.

4. Place rice, chickpeas, broth, paprika, saffron (if using), and salt in a deep saucepan or stockpot. Bring to a boil and cook, uncovered, 10 minutes.

5. Pour rice mixture into a baking dish (about 12 inches square). Arrange sausage, potatoes, and tomatoes on top of the rice, placing garlic in the center. Cover with aluminum foil and bake 25 minutes, or until liquid is nearly absorbed.

6. Remove from oven and allow to sit, still covered, 10 minutes. Uncover and serve from baking dish. (Do not serve garlic.)

Preparation time: 20 minutes
Cooking time: 1 hour
Serves 4 to 6

Norma's Pasta / *Pasta alla Norma* (Italy)

This classic Sicilian dish is a specialty in Catania, a city on the island's northeastern coast. It is said to have been named in honor of Vincenzo Bellini, a Catania native who composed the famous opera Norma in about 1831.

2 eggplants, cut into slices ¼-inch thick

1 tbsp. plus ¾ tsp. plus 1 tbsp. salt

3 tbsp. plus 1½ tbsp. olive oil

1 small yellow onion, chopped

3 cloves garlic, minced

6 to 8 fresh tomatoes, peeled* and diced, or 28 oz. canned diced tomatoes

pinch sugar

¼ tsp. crushed red pepper (optional)

¼ tsp. pepper

4 tbsp. fresh basil, chopped, or 2 tbsp. dried basil

1 lb. spaghetti, penne, or other pasta

⅓ c. ricotta salata, grated**

1. Sprinkle the sliced eggplant with 1 tbsp. salt and place in a colander. Set aside for at least 30 minutes.

2. Rinse eggplant slices well in cool running water and pat dry with paper towels.

3. In a skillet or frying pan, heat 3 tbsp. of the olive oil over medium-high heat. Place as many eggplant slices as fit comfortably in the pan and fry 2 minutes on each side or until golden brown. Repeat with remaining slices. Set aside on paper towels and cover with an extra towel to keep warm.

4. In a saucepan or deep skillet, heat remaining 1½ tbsp. olive oil over medium-high heat and sauté onion 4 to 6 minutes. Add garlic and sauté another 3 to 4 minutes, or until onion and garlic are soft but not brown. Reduce heat to low and carefully add tomatoes to pan. Stir in sugar, crushed red pepper (if using), ¾ tsp. salt, and black pepper. Add dried basil (if using).

5. Cook uncovered for 25 minutes, stirring occasionally, or until sauce has thickened.

6. While sauce is cooking, fill a saucepan or stockpot about three-fourths full of water. Sprinkle in 1 tbsp. salt and bring to a boil. Add pasta and cook for the length of time specified in the package directions.

7. While both sauce and pasta are cooking, cut eggplant slices into bite-sized pieces.

8. Check pasta for tenderness. When done, remove from heat and carefully pour into a large colander. Run cool water over pasta to stop the cooking process.

9. When sauce has thickened, add pasta, eggplant, and fresh basil (if using) and mix well. Ladle into a large serving bowl and sprinkle with ricotta salata. Serve immediately.

*See p. 42 for a tip on peeling tomatoes.

**Look for ricotta salata, which is dried, salted ricotta, in specialty Italian markets. If you can't find it, you can substitute grated Parmesan or Romano or even crumbled feta cheese. The taste won't be quite the same, but you're still sure to love it!

Preparation time: 15 minutes
(plus 30 minutes resting time)
Cooking time: 1 to 1¼ hours
Serves 4 to 6

Chicken and Apricot Stew / Tagine bi Dajaaj (North Africa)

Warm, filling tagines—named for the earthenware pot in which they were traditionally cooked—are one of the most typically North African dishes.

4 tbsp. olive oil

2 lb. skinless, boneless chicken breasts and thighs*

2 small yellow onions, 1 chopped and 1 sliced

1 clove garlic, minced

1 stick or 1 tsp. ground cinnamon

½ tsp. turmeric

2 tsp. salt

1 tsp. pepper

pinch saffron (optional)

3 tbsp. honey

1 c. dried apricots, soaked in water overnight

couscous, prepared according to package directions

After handling raw chicken or other poultry, always remember to thoroughly wash your hands, utensils, and preparation area with hot, soapy water. Also, when checking chicken for doneness, it's a good idea to cut it open gently to make sure that the meat is white (not pink) all the way through.

**For an extra crunch, sauté ¼ c. slivered almonds in 1 tbsp. of butter and sprinkle over tagine before serving.*

1. In a large stockpot, heat olive oil over medium-high heat. Add chicken, the chopped onion, and garlic, and sauté 4 to 6 minutes, or until chicken pieces have begun to brown on all sides and onions are soft.

2. Pour about 1 c. of water into pot and add sliced onions, cinnamon, turmeric, salt, pepper, and saffron (if using). Stir well. Add more water until chicken is just covered.

3. Raise heat to high and bring to a boil. Cover, reduce heat, and simmer 1 hour, or until chicken is tender and cooked all the way through.

4. Remove chicken pieces to a platter. Add honey and apricots to the pot, stir well and simmer 15 to 20 minutes more, or until sauce begins to thicken. Return chicken to pot and heat through.

5. Remove cinnamon stick (if using) and serve tagine hot, with couscous.**

Preparation time: 10 minutes
(plus overnight soaking time)
Cooking time: 1½ to 1¾ hours
Serves 4 to 6

Stuffed Grape Leaves/Dolmádes
(Albania, Greece, Turkey, Middle East)

In the eastern Mediterranean, grape leaves for this recipe are usually picked right off the vine and used that same day. Even if you use bottled grape leaves, you can still enjoy a plate of these delectable little packets, which can be served as a main course or as an appetizer for a larger group of people.

½ lb. lean ground beef, lamb, pork, or a combination*

1 small white or yellow onion, chopped

1 clove garlic, minced

½ c. uncooked long-grain white rice

2 or 3 green onions, chopped

½ c. fresh dill, chopped, or 4 tbsp. dried dill

¼ c. fresh mint and/or parsley, chopped, or 2 tbsp. dried mint and/or parsley (optional)

2 tsp. pepper

4 tbsp. olive oil, divided in half

6 tbsp. lemon juice, divided in half

1 8-oz. jar grape leaves

1. In a large mixing bowl, combine all ingredients except for half of the olive oil, half of the lemon juice, and the grape leaves. Mix well, using your hands if necessary to blend all ingredients together. If the mixture is too dry to be workable, add 1 or 2 tbsp. water.

2. Carefully remove grape leaves from jar and separate leaves from each other. Gently rinse each leaf in cool water.

3. Lay a leaf flat, with the shiny side down, on a clean countertop or other work surface. Place about 1 tbsp. of rice-meat filling near the stem end of the leaf. Fold the 2 sides over the filling and then fold over the stem end of the leaf. Roll from the stem end toward the tip of the leaf and press the edges of the leaf lightly to seal. Set roll, seam-side down, in a wide saucepan, stockpot, or deep skillet with a lid.

4. Repeat with remaining filling and grape leaves and continue to place rolls in pan, forming a loosely packed layer. When one layer is complete, sprinkle 1 tbsp. of the remaining olive oil and 2 tbsp. of the remaining lemon juice over rolls before beginning the next layer. When all rolls have been made, sprinkle the rest of the oil and lemon juice over all.

5. Pour enough water over the rolls to almost cover them. Place lid on pan and cook over low heat. Simmer 45 minutes to 1 hour, or until the water has been absorbed and the rolls are tender. Serve cold or at room temperature, with lemon wedges and tzatziki (see recipe on p. 33).

*For a vegetarian version, simply replace the meat with an extra ½ c. rice. If you like, you can also add pine nuts for extra texture and flavor. Place 2 tbsp. pine nuts in a small skillet and cook over medium heat, stirring often to prevent burning. Cook 4 to 6 minutes, or until lightly browned. Add pine nuts to the mixture in Step 1.

Preparation time: 1 hour
Cooking time: 45 minutes to 1 hour
Serves 4 to 6

Blintzes (Israel)

Depending on the filling—which can be sweet or savory—these traditional Jewish pancakes can make a hearty breakfast, a light dinner, or a rich dessert.* If you use more than one of the fillings below, reduce the filling recipes or increase your batter recipe.

Potato filling:

3 medium potatoes

1 tbsp. olive oil

1 large yellow onion, chopped

½ tsp. salt

¼ tsp. pepper

1. Place potatoes in a pot with enough water to cover. Bring to a boil and cook for 20 to 25 minutes, or until very tender. Drain in a colander. Once potatoes have cooled, peel and mash with a large fork.

2. Place oil in a skillet and add onion. Sauté 3 or 4 minutes, or until onion is soft but not brown. Remove from heat.

3. In a large mixing bowl, combine potatoes, onion, salt, and pepper. Mix well.

Basic cheese filling:

1 c. nonfat or low-fat cottage cheese

8 oz. cream cheese, softened

1 egg, beaten

2 tbsp. sugar

¼ tsp. salt

4 tbsp. raisins (optional)

dash cinnamon (optional)

1. Combine all ingredients in a medium-sized mixing bowl.

2. Beat until smooth.

*For a sweet treat, try filling your blintzes with chocolate sauce. Serve with a sprinkling of powdered sugar.

Batter:

1 tbsp. butter, melted

2 eggs

1 c. milk

½ tsp. salt

1 c. all-purpose flour

butter or margarine for greasing pan
    plus 2 tbsp. for frying

**If you like, serve cheese blintzes with applesauce and potato blintzes with sour cream.

1. In a large mixing bowl, combine butter, eggs, and milk. Beat well. Turn off mixer and slowly add salt and flour, stirring with a spoon or whisk to keep lumps from forming.

2. Lightly grease a small (7- to 9-inch) nonstick skillet or frying pan with butter. Place over medium-high heat until the butter is bubbling but not browning. Using a ladle, place about ¼ c. batter into pan. Swirl pan to cover surface with a thin, even layer of batter. Cook 2 to 3 minutes, or until the blintz looks dry and the surface begins to bubble.

3. Use a spatula to remove blintz to a paper towel. Continue with remaining batter. If batter begins sticking, melt a bit more butter in the pan.

4. When finished, lay a blintz on a flat work surface. Place about 2 tbsp. filling in the blintz's center and roll it up, tucking the open ends underneath the roll. The roll should be about 4 inches long. Repeat with remaining blintzes and filling.

5. Melt 2 tbsp. butter in skillet over medium-high heat and fry each blintz 2 to 3 minutes on each side, or until golden brown and lightly crispy. Serve hot.**

Preparation time: 25 minutes
Cooking time: 1½ hours
Serves 6 to 8

Desserts and Drinks

Nearly every Mediterranean diner looks forward to a little something sweet at the end of a meal. Most often this dessert is as simple as a piece of the fresh fruit that is so abundant in the region. But regional cooks are also experts at preparing richer and more elaborate sweets. North African desserts, such as the date-filled makroudh, are often heavy and intensely sweet. The northern Mediterranean also features a host of specialty sweets, which tend to be richer in dairy products. Sicily claims to be the original home of cannoli, pastry shells filled with sweetened ricotta cheese.

Regional beverages are also an important element of Mediterranean meals and can be sweet or salty. Sweet mint tea is served in every North African home, and cold, slightly salty ayran is a perfect summer drink in the eastern Mediterranean.

Italian cannoli provide a sweet way to end a Mediterranean meal. (Recipe on page 61.)

Date-Filled Pastries/Makroudh (North Africa)

These traditionally diamond-shaped desserts are a favorite in Tunisia, Libya, and Algeria.

Dough:

3 c. semolina flour*

¼ tsp. salt

pinch baking soda

2 sticks (1 c.) unsalted butter,
  melted and slightly cooled

¼ to ½ c. warm water

Filling:

2 c. pitted, finely chopped dates

½ tsp. cinnamon

rind of 1 orange, finely chopped
  (optional)**

1 tbsp. vegetable oil

Syrup:

1 c. honey

½ c. water

vegetable oil for frying

1. In a large mixing bowl, combine semolina, salt, and baking soda. Slowly stir in melted butter and mix well, using your hands if necessary. Test mixture's texture by rolling a small amount into a ball. If the dough is crumbly, add another tsp. or so of melted butter or vegetable oil.

2. Place dough on a clean and floured countertop or other work surface. Sprinkle dough with 1 tsp. of the warm water and knead lightly until dough has a soft, smooth, and slightly stretchy texture. Add extra water if dough feels dry and does not hold together. Return dough to bowl, cover with a damp kitchen towel, and set aside for 15 minutes.

3. While dough is resting, make filling. In the bowl of a food processor, place dates, cinnamon, and orange rind (if using). Pulse a few seconds to mix, add oil, and pulse until mixture is pastelike. (If you don't have a food processor, you can use a blender or mash the mixture with a mortar and pestle.) Set aside.

4. On a clean and floured countertop or other work surface, divide dough in half. Form one half into a loaf about 3 inches wide. Use your fingertips or the back of a spoon to press a deep groove along the loaf's center. Fill the groove with about half of the date filling. Fold sides of loaf over filling, pinching to seal and smoothing the seam with your fingers. Cut loaf at a diagonal into slices about 1½ inches wide. Repeat with remaining dough and filling.

5. In a small saucepan, combine honey and water. Stir well and leave to warm over very low heat. Meanwhile, pour vegetable oil about ½-inch deep in a skillet or saucepan. Drop in pastry slices a few at a time and fry 2 to 3 minutes on each side, or until golden brown.*** Set aside to drain on paper towels.

6. Dip makroudh in warm honey syrup and place on a serving platter. Serve cool.

Preparation time: 40 to 45 minutes
(plus 15 minutes resting time)
Cooking time: 40 to 45 minutes
Makes 25 to 30 pastries

*Semolina is a coarsely ground wheat flour. Check for it at your local grocery store, coop, or supermarket.

**Use a potato peeler or a zester to gently remove peel in small strips from the orange. Try to avoid getting the white part, which has a bitter taste. Chop or mince the peel with a knife for even smaller pieces.

***To lower the fat content of these pastries, spread them on baking sheets instead of stove top frying and bake at 375°F for 40 minutes, or until golden brown.

Yogurt Drink/Ayran (Turkey)

This beverage is a welcome refreshment on a hot Turkish day.

4 c. plain yogurt

3½ to 4½ c. water

1½ tsp. salt

*For a twist on basic ayran, try adding 1 tbsp. dried or 2 tbsp. fresh, chopped mint or ¼ c. lemon juice before blending.

1. Combine yogurt, water, and salt in a blender.* (Vary the amount of water depending on how thick you want the drink to be.) Blend until frothy.

2. Serve with ice.

Preparation time: 5 minutes
Serves 4

Mint Tea/Thé à la Menthe, Etzai, or Atay (North Africa and Middle East)

Mint tea is the classic beverage of North Africa and the Middle East. It is typically enjoyed after, between, and sometimes with meals. It won't be the same without fresh mint, so try to find a bunch at your grocery store or supermarket.

1½ tbsp. green tea

1 bunch fresh mint leaves, washed well

12 to 15 sugar cubes, or 3 to 4 tbsp. sugar*

3 c. boiling water

*You may use more or less sugar, depending on how sweet you like your tea.

1. Rinse a small teapot with hot or boiling water and pour water out. Place tea, mint, and sugar in teapot and refill with 3 c. boiling water.

2. Leave tea to steep for 5 minutes. Pour through a strainer into small heat-resistant glasses and serve hot.

Preparation time: 10 minutes
Serves 4 to 6

Mediterranean Fruit Salad

A wealth of fresh fruit is one of the Mediterranean's greatest treasures, and dessert in many of the region's countries can be as simple as a bowl of berries or a fig plucked right from the family's tree. This recipe is just a guideline—feel free to create your salad in the true Mediterranean spirit by using your favorite fruits of the season.

1 melon, such as honeydew or cantaloupe

2 pears

2 apples

2 oranges

½ lb. strawberries

1 medium bunch red or green grapes

1. Wash all fruit well.

2. Cut honeydew or cantaloupe in half and scoop out seeds with a small spoon. Slice melon, pears, and apples into bite-sized pieces. Peel oranges and divide into sections. Remove the green top and center core from the strawberries and cut berries in half. Remove grapes from stem.

3. Combine all fruit in a large bowl and mix gently.*

Preparation time: 15 minutes
Serves 4 to 6

*For a Middle Eastern flavor, try sprinkling 1 or 2 tbsp. finely chopped almonds over fruit. Or for an Italian taste, toss fruit with 3 tbsp. lemon juice and 1 tbsp. sugar. For a Greek or Turkish flair, add 1 tsp. of cinnamon and 1 tbsp. honey.

Cannoli (Italy)

Bakeries throughout Sicily and southern Italy serve freshly made cannoli to passersby with a sweet tooth. Although many Italian cooks make their own cannoli shells using special metal molds, you can buy shells already made at many grocery stores and Italian markets. Filling the crunchy shells just before serving keeps them from getting soggy.

2 c. ricotta cheese*

⅓ c. powdered sugar plus additional for sprinkling

1 tsp. vanilla extract

2 tbsp. candied orange peel, finely chopped, or 2 tbsp. grated fresh orange peel

4 tbsp. mini chocolate chips

12 small cannoli shells (about 2 to 3 inches long)

¼ c. pistachios, finely chopped

1. Place ricotta in a colander in the sink and let it drain for 30 minutes.

2. In a large mixing bowl, combine ricotta and powdered sugar. Beat with an electric mixer until smooth and creamy. Stir in vanilla, orange peel, and chocolate chips. Cover and refrigerate until ready to serve.**

3. Using a pastry bag or a small spoon or knife, fill a cannoli shell with ricotta mixture. Start by filling from one end of the shell and then finish from the other end, being careful not to break shell. Repeat with remaining shells and filling.

4. Sprinkle ends of cannoli with pistachios, and using a small sifter, sprinkle powdered sugar over each cannoli. Serve immediately.

*Preparation time: 35 to 45 minutes
(plus 30 minutes draining time)
Makes 12 small cannoli*

*Fresh ricotta, sold in Italian specialty stores, is typically watery and needs to be drained. However, if you buy packaged ricotta from a supermarket, you can skip Step 1.

**To make cannoli with a chocolate filling, add 2 tsp. powdered cocoa in Step 2.

Holiday and Festival Food

In the Mediterranean, every meal can be a special occasion. Regional cooks take pride in their fresh ingredients, their family recipes, and their local specialties. But holidays and other celebrations are cause for extra care, as well as a host of favorite dishes traditionally associated with those celebrations.

The area's historical dependence on agriculture put farmers and families at the mercy of the seasons and the success of yearly crops. As a result, celebrations giving thanks for a bountiful harvest and asking for future abundance are a major part of Mediterranean festivals. Other important events are religious holidays, which encompass Islam, Judaism, and Christianity. Many of the dishes prepared for these events are eaten in several of the region's nations, but individual countries often have their own twists on the shared recipes. Prepare the dishes in this section yourself for a taste of celebrating the Mediterranean way.

These buttery Greek holiday cookies are favorites at a wide variety of celebrations. (Recipe on page 64.)

Holiday Cookies/Kourabiéthes (Greece)

These light, flaky cookies are eaten in Greece for Easter, Christmas, weddings, birthdays, and just about every other special occasion. At Christmas they are often topped with whole cloves.

1 c. (2 sticks) unsalted butter at room temperature

½ c. powdered sugar plus additional for dusting

2 tsp. vanilla extract

1 tbsp. milk

1 egg

2¼ c. flour

¼ tsp. baking powder

¼ tsp. salt

¾ c. slivered almonds, toasted*

1. Preheat oven to 350°F.

2. In a large mixing bowl, combine butter and powdered sugar. Using an electric mixer, cream together until very light and fluffy, about 5 minutes.

3. Add vanilla extract, milk, and egg. Mix well. Measure flour, baking powder, and salt into a sifter and sift over egg mixture. Beat well until thoroughly blended. Stir in toasted almonds.

4. With a spoon, scoop up 1 to 2 tsp. of dough. Use your hands to form it into a ball, crescent, or S-shape.** Place on an ungreased baking sheet. Continue with remaining dough, leaving about 2 inches between cookies. Bake 20 minutes, or until light golden brown.

5. Remove from oven and allow to cool for 15 minutes. Spread powdered sugar on a plate or in shallow bowl. Roll cookies in sugar before storing in airtight container.

*To toast almonds, place them in a medium skillet and cook over medium heat, stirring often to prevent burning. Cook 4 to 6 minutes, or until lightly browned.

**If dough seems exceptionally soft or sticky (a very warm kitchen or humid weather could cause this), cover bowl in plastic wrap and place in refrigerator for up to 1 hour.

Preparation time: 45 minutes
Baking time: 20 minutes
Makes about 4 dozen cookies

Couscous with Butter/
Couscous au Beurre (Algeria and Morocco)

Although couscous is popular all across French-speaking North Africa, this sweet version is less common. Traditionally served by Jews living in Algeria and Morocco for holidays, including Passover and Hanukkah, this dish can be a light—though very sweet—main course or a dessert.

2¼ c. water

¼ tsp. salt

2 c. quick-cooking couscous

½ to 1 tbsp. oil

⅓ c. raisins, dark or golden

2 to 3 tbsp. butter, cut into cubes

2½ tbsp. sugar

1 tbsp. cinnamon (optional)

*Some cooks like to add ⅓ c. or so of slivered almonds at this point. Try this variation for a bit of crunch in your couscous.

**If desired, serve each guest a glass of mint tea and a small dish of buttermilk or yogurt to enjoy alongside the couscous.

1. In a medium saucepan, bring water and salt to a boil. Remove from heat and stir in couscous. Cover and let sit for 5 minutes, or until water has been absorbed.

2. Add enough oil to coat couscous grains very lightly and mix with a fork.

3. Heat a few cups of water in a wide, shallow pot over medium heat. Place covered saucepan of couscous in the pot to steam.

4. Add raisins. Mix well, replace cover, and steam 10 minutes longer.

5. Carefully remove saucepan from heat. Add butter to couscous and toss mixture to break up any lumps.*

6. Pour couscous into a wide, shallow serving bowl, or onto a platter. Form the mound of couscous into a rough cone shape and sprinkle sugar and cinnamon (if using) over all.**

Preparation time: 10 minutes
Cooking time: 25 miutes
Serves 4 to 6

Cheese and Melon/Halloumi me Peponi (Cyprus)

This very popular dish shows up on Cypriot tables during summertime watermelon harvest festivals. The unusual combination of flavors is sure to give your taste buds a surprising treat. Diners can nibble on the different foods one at a time or mix them together, as they prefer.

2 tbsp. olive oil

8 oz. halloumi cheese, sliced about ¼-inch thick*

4 slices watermelon, cut into quarters**

6 pieces pita bread, cut into quarters

1. Place olive oil in a medium skillet and heat over medium heat. Add as many halloumi slices as will fit easily and cook 2 minutes, or until lightly browned. Flip each slice with a spatula and brown other side. Remove cheese to a plate and repeat with remaining slices.

2. Arrange halloumi slices, watermelon slices, and pita bread alongside each other on a platter and serve.

Preparation time: 15 minutes
Cooking time: 10 to 15 minutes
Serves 4 to 6

*Look for halloumi at your grocery store or supermarket, or at Greek, Turkish, or Middle Eastern specialty shops. If you can't find it, most other goat's or sheep's milk cheeses are good substitutes. Fresh mozzarella can also be used.

**Ask an adult to help you cut the watermelon, or look for precut slices at the grocery store.

Meat and Lentil Soup/Harira (North Africa)

Moroccan Muslims fasting during Ramadan look forward to dining on this hearty soup after sunset.

2 tbsp. olive oil

½ lb. lean chicken, lamb, or beef, cubed*

2 cloves garlic, minced

2 medium white onions, chopped

1 stalk celery, chopped

½ tsp. ground turmeric

1 tsp. cinnamon

¼ tsp. ground ginger

1 tsp. black pepper

1 tsp. salt

6 c. chicken or beef stock

¾ c. dried red lentils, soaked overnight

16 oz. canned tomatoes, chopped, or 1½ lb. fresh tomatoes, peeled, seeded, and chopped

¼ c. fresh cilantro, chopped, plus sprigs for garnish

¼ c. fresh parsley, chopped, plus sprigs for garnish

¾ c. canned chickpeas, drained

1 c. uncooked rice or angel hair pasta, broken into small pieces

1 egg, beaten with the juice of 1 lemon

1 lemon, cut into thin wedges, to garnish

1. Heat olive oil in a large stockpot over medium heat. Add meat and sauté 5 minutes or until lightly browned on all sides. Add garlic, onions, celery, turmeric, cinnamon, ginger, black pepper, and salt. Stir well and sauté 5 minutes longer. Remove meat to a platter and set aside.

2. Add stock to pot and bring to a boil. Drain lentils and rinse well. Add lentils and meat to pot. Reduce heat to medium. Cover and simmer 1 hour.

3. Add tomatoes, cilantro, and parsley. Simmer uncovered 20 minutes longer, stirring occasionally. If soup looks too thick, add 1 c. water.

4. Add chickpeas and pasta or rice. Simmer 20 minutes, or until all ingredients are tender. Stir in beaten egg and lemon juice, cook 1 minute longer, and serve immediately. Garnish with lemon wedges, cilantro, and parsley.

*Preparation time: 30 minutes
(plus overnight soaking time)
Cooking time: 2 hours
Serves 4 to 6*

*To create a vegetarian harira, omit the meat, double the amount of lentils and chickpeas, and use water or vegetable stock instead of chicken or beef stock.

Index

About the Authors

Alison Behnke is an author and editor of children's books. She enjoys traveling and experiencing new cultures and cuisines. Among her other cookbooks are *Cooking the Cuban Way*, *Cooking the Middle Eastern Way*, and *Vegetarian Cooking around the World*. She has also written geography books, including *Italy in Pictures* and *Afghanistan in Pictures*.

Anna and Lazaros Christoforides own Gardens of Salonica, a Greek restaurant in Minneapolis, Minnesota. From a modest seven-table start, they built their restaurant into an award-winning and popular favorite, specializing in simple, traditional recipes.

Photo Acknowledgments
The photographs in this book are reproduced with permission of: © Sergio Pitamitz/CORBIS, p. 2-3; © Walter and Louiseann Pietrowicz/September 8th Stock, pp. 4 (both), 5 (both), 6, 18, 30, 34, 37, 40, 43, 44, 49, 54, 59, 62, 67, 68; © Geray Sweeney/CORBIS, p. 10; © Craig Aurness/CORBIS, p. 13; © Richard T. Nowitz/CORBIS, p. 16; © David Turnley/CORBIS, p. 26.

Cover photos (front, back, and spine): © Walter and Louiseann Pietrowicz/ September 8th Stock.

The illustrations on pages 7, 19, 27, 31, 32, 33, 35, 36, 39, 41, 42, 45, 47, 48, 51, 52, 53, 55, 57, 58, 60, 61, 63, 64, 65, 66, and 69 are by Tim Seeley. The map on page 8 is by Bill Hauser.